LOVE, 50 WAYS

Fun Yet Scientifically-Proven Ways to Connect with Your Lover

By Matthew Driggs

introduction

I can still picture my beautiful wife dressed in white with a huge smile and innocence
in her eyes as we looked across the church alter and shared promises to love each other
for the rest of our lives. She is as beautiful now as she was 25 years ago. Sure, we have
had our challenges, beginning with the day after our wedding as we drove to Palm
Springs for our honeymoon. Two hours into the drive, my wife burst into tears because
she missed her family. I was too young and naïve to see that my bride was someone who
loved deeply and that she had chosen me to give that love to. I see now how lucky I am
to be the recipient of that love.

Marriage is a leap of faith for all of us. We say, "I do" then hope our sweetheart makes
us happy. There are no manuals that guarantee a perfect marriage and even if there
were, we often think, "Who needs a manual when love fixes everything?"

After 25 years of being in love, I now know that love doesn't fix everything. Many
divorced couples still love their exes; they just couldn't stand living with them. Our
happiness with our spouse is made up of little choices every day that either build or
tear down our relationship. Luckily, all of us in successful marriages stumble upon
a few good tactics that cement our relationship and keep those feelings of love and
commitment burning bright.

I am so fortunate to have a wife who is always looking for ways to strengthen our marriage. Our passion to become the best, happiest couple has lead me to look at thousands of relationship studies to find the most effective and easiest activities that are scientifically proven to bring couples closer together. The following is a compilation of what I think are the top 50 ideas that will actually make you happier, healthier, more connected and will take your love to new heights. Best of all, these activities are fun and easy to do. Keep in mind that these studies represent averages and not every single activity will work for your relationship. Just keep trying and have fun together as you work towards the relationship you have always dreamed of.

I also want to give a huge shout out to all those individuals on the front lines that are actually doing this research at universities throughout the world. It is through their efforts that all of us can more effectively build our relationships. Thank you so much for contributing to the happiness I have found in my marriage.

I am hopeful that these 50 ideas help increase the love and compassion in your relationship. I am having fun with my wife working on them. I suspect that I am much like many of you when I express my heartfelt gratitude to my sweetheart for putting her faith in me and for choosing me to be her eternal companion. Ali, you are the best thing that has ever happened to me.

—*Matthew Driggs*

01

time travel

Let's begin with an easy one: time travel. Well, not literally—although that would make a great date. But we're talking about reminiscing, going back to the moments where you both first fell in love. Studies show that reliving your best memories together helps strengthen your relationship.[1]

Look at some old snapshots, talk about some of your favorite dates and moments together, things you value most about each other and the minute you first knew you were in love. Travel through time and fall in love all over again.

Make a list of some of your favorite early memories, then plan a date that takes you there. Remember your old favorite songs, outdated fashion choices, favorite foods or even your go-to make out spot.

[1] Bryant, F. B., Smart, C. M., & King, S. P. (2005). Using the Past to Enhance the Present: Boosting Happiness Through Positive Reminiscence. Journal of Happiness Studies J Happiness Study.

02

get a move on

Research shows that the more time couples spend together doing fun activities they both enjoy, the happier and more satisfied they are in the relationship.[2]

Having a hard time coming up with ideas? Check out the list on the following page of fun and engaging activities. Find something you are both interested in and give it a try.

Once a month choose an activity on the list, put it on your calendar and do something fun together. See how many different activities you can do this year.

[2] Girme, Y. U., Overall, N. C., & Faingataa, S. (2013). "Date nights" take two: The maintenance function of shared relationship activities. Pers Relationship Personal Relationships.

1. Frisbee golf
2. 5K runs: Mud Run, Color Run, etc.
3. Mini golf, driving range, Topgolf
4. Rock climbing, rockhounding
5. Street hockey
6. Ice skating
7. Cave exploring
8. Skydiving – indoor or outdoor
9. Park – walks, fly kites, ice blocking
10. Boating, jet skiing, waterskiing
11. Tennis, pickle ball, racquetball
12. River rafting, tubing
13. Alpine slide
14. Ziplining
15. Swimming – indoor or outdoor
16. Beach, sand dunes
17. 4-wheeling, offroading
18. Roller skating
19. Bounce houses
20. Waterparks
21. Go-karts
22. Family fun center
23. Paintballing
24. Archery shooting
25. Batting cages
26. Bike rides, mountain biking
27. Hiking, walking
28. Fishing
29. Bowling
30. Camping
31. Horseback riding
32. Trampoline park
33. Amusement park
34. Sports – basketball, baseball, dodgeball
35. Sledding, tubing
36. Skiing, night skiing
37. Snowmobiling
38. Snorkeling or scuba diving
39. Shooting, hunting, gun safety course
40. Hot air balloon ride

03

love letters

Researchers at Indiana University conducted studies to determine the effects of writing gratitude letters. For three weeks, participants spent 20 minutes writing one letter each week expressing their gratitude. Three months later, brain scans demonstrated increased activity in the parts of the brain that control empathy and sensitivity towards others, compared with individuals who did not write the gratitude letters.[3]

This study also showed that the more you express and show gratitude, the more grateful you become. These "gratitude muscles" get stronger the more you use them. Long after love letters are mailed, they can still be read, appreciated and preserved. They are permanent reminders of our love for each other.

Surprise your sweetheart with a love note sent by special delivery or put the note in a special place.

[3] Kini, P., Wong, J., Mcinnis, S., Gabana, N., & Brown, J. W. (2016). The effects of gratitude expression on neural activity. NeuroImage.

04

dress to
the nines

Looks aren't everything, but they certainly say a lot. In fact, appearance affects others in such a way that by simply looking nice, we are perceived as kinder, more sensitive, outgoing, interesting and even wealthier.[4] This simple act of dressing up really makes us seem more awesome.

While there's no need to change out of our sweats for a lazy weekend, a little effort in an outfit for a special day can make a big difference in your relationship.

Surprise your lover with a new outfit for your next date and see the sparks fly when you're both dressed to the nines.

[4] Dion, K., Berscheid, E., & Walster, E. (1972). What is beautiful is good. Journal of Personality and Social Psychology.

05

the couple's bucket list

One of the best things you can do for your relationship is share amazing experiences together.[5] Not surprisingly, boredom is a strong indication of relationship decline.[6] To avoid this decline, some might want to make the time to finally go skydiving. For others, it's finding time to break out those golden pipes during karaoke at the local bar.

Whether or not you and your loved one are adventurous, think about some activities you've always wanted to try: some easy and close to home, and some outrageous outings to look forward to doing together. You'll have fun just in the anticipation.[7] Now go out and make some memories with your favorite sidekick.

1. Write the ultimate to-do list together with your partner, or each write your own and pick activities from each.

2. Write a completion date next to a few of the activities that you are really excited to do.

3. Keep the list in a place where you both will see and talk about it often.

[5] Reissman, C., Aron, A., & Bergen, M. R. (1993). Shared Activities and Marital Satisfaction: Causal Direction and Self-Expansion versus Boredom. Journal of Social and Personal Relationships.

[6] Tsapelas, I., Aron, A., & Orbuch, T. (2009). Marital Boredom Now Predicts Less Satisfaction 9 Years Later. Psychological Science.

[7] Nawijn, J., Marchand, M. A., Veenhoven, R., & Vingerhoets, A. J. (2010). Vacationers Happier, but Most not Happier After a Holiday. Applied Research Quality Life Applied Research in Quality of Life.

06

make me laugh

Everyone wants to be with someone who has a good sense of humor.[8] Sharing something funny is a great way to add a little charm and happiness into your relationship.[9] Humor helps people succeed in intimate relationships because it allows couples to better handle the stress within the relationship.[10]

It should come as no big surprise that happier couples report higher instances of positive humor with lower levels of negative humor in their relationship. When you share something funny with your partner, they see that you are thinking of them and it is a great way to bring smiles and laughter into your home.

While you're at work or on the go, find a funny joke, story or picture and randomly share it with your partner. Try attaching a sweet note so they know you're thinking of them.

[8] Cowan, M. L., & Little, A. C. (2013). The effects of relationship context and modality on ratings of funniness. Personality and Individual Differences.

[9] Hampes, W. P. (1992). Relation Between Intimacy And Humor. Psychological Reports.

[10] Butzer, B., & Kuiper, N. A. (2008). Humor Use in Romantic Relationships: The Effects of Relationship. Satisfaction and Pleasant Versus Conflict Situations. The Journal of Psychology.

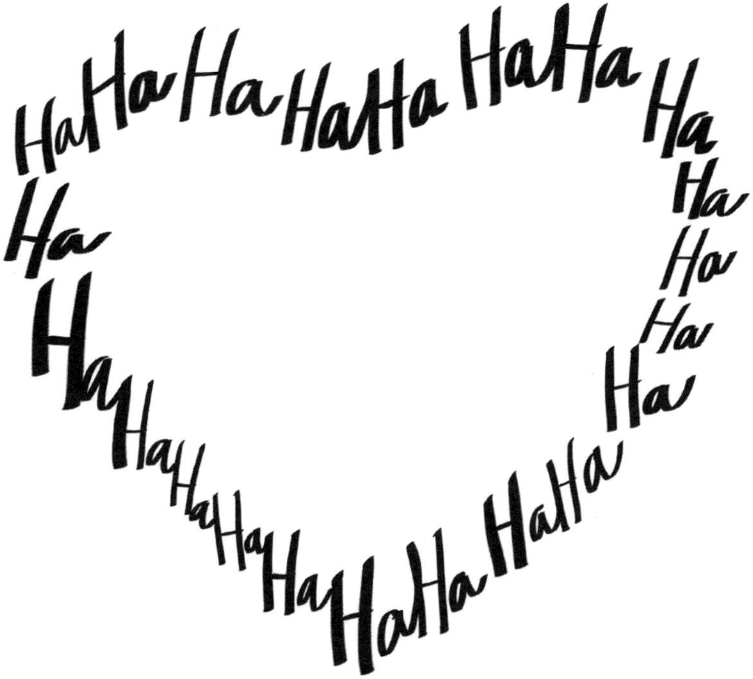
HaHa Ha HaHa HaHa
Ha Ha Ha Ha Ha
HaHa HaHa
Ha Ha Ha Ha
Ha Ha

07

a deeper double date

We've all been on double dates, but did you know forming a friendship with another couple actually improves your own relationship? Taking your relationship to the next level involves more than just small talk, but a thing called "high self-disclosure dialogue." Being a little vulnerable really pays off.

In a recent study, when couples spent time discussing deeper topics, ones that showed vulnerability, not only did couples increase their social support group, but they actually felt closer to their own partners for months to come.[11] Make your date more interesting by talking about things like how you first met, your most embarrassing moments or the things you are most grateful for in life.

Plan a night out with another couple and dig a little deeper in your conversations.

---

[11] Slatcher, R. B. (2010). When Harry and Sally met Dick and Jane: Creating closeness between couples.

08

take an "ussie"

Admittedly, when you take a selfie, it's kind of all about you. Why not mix it up and make it all about us? Science confirms that couples who have more "we" identity have more satisfaction, intimacy and commitment in their relationship.[12]

Additionally when couples share fun moments together and memorialize it in the photo, they increase their emotional intimacy, trust and satisfaction in their relationship. Each photo of you as a couple shows the world that you are in love and committed to each other.

Next time you're doing something fun and exciting together, take out your phone, take a snap of you two and share it on social media for all to see.

[12] Aron, A., Aron, E. N., & Smollan, D. (1992). Inclusion of Other in the Self Scale and the structure of interpersonal closeness. Journal of Personality and Social Psychology.

09

let your emotions shine

By holding back your emotions, you do more harm than good. It may come as no surprise that it's not just damaging to you, but to your relationship. Researchers watched couples as they discussed sacrifices for their relationship and counted how often couples shared their true feelings. Couples who didn't share how they truly felt, experienced more negative emotions, more conflict, more thoughts of breaking up and greater dissatisfaction in their relationship.[13]

Partners who can let go of being "right" and make the difficult jump toward true empathy make their relationship stronger in the long run.[14] It makes sense that you don't want to focus on the negative; however, research makes it clear that you actually harm the relationship more when you don't share how you feel.

Next time you struggle with difficult feelings, don't bury them. Take a chance and share how you are feeling with your partner.

[13] Impett, E. A., Kogan, A., English, T., John, O., Oveis, C., Gordon, A. M., & Keltner, D. (2012). Suppression Sours Sacrifice: Emotional and Relational Costs of Suppressing Emotions in Romantic Relationships. Personality and Social Psychology Bulletin.

[14] Gordon, A. M., & Chen, S. (2016). Do you get where I'm coming from?: Perceived understanding buffers against the negative impact of conflict on relationship satisfaction. Journal of Personality and Social Psychology.

10

flower power

Roses, daisies, peonies—almost everyone loves flowers, whether they realize it or not, it's actually proven. In one study, women rated men sexier and more attractive who sat in a room with flowers, compared to no flowers.[15]

In another study, men who stood near a flower shop were twice as likely to successfully get phone numbers of random women passing by. Moral of the study – have flowers around to beautify your home and your lover.[16]

Surprise your special someone with a bouquet of beautiful flowers. Consider starting a tradition like "Flower Fridays" and make having flowers around a priority—trust me, it'll be worth it.

[15] Guéguen, N. (2011). "Say it with flowers": The effect of flowers on mating attractiveness and behavior. Social Influence.

[16] Guéguen, N. (2012). "Say it … Near the Flower Shop": Further Evidence of the Effect of Flowers.

II

turn up the heat with hot foods

Our physical enivornment can play a big role in the way we feel about our lover. Being outside on a chilly day eating ice cream can actually make you feel cold towards your partner. Warm foods such as soups, hot chocolate, or warm rolls actually heat up attraction.[17]

The next time you want to warm up your relationship, start with warming up your food. When you share something warm, or even spicy, your attraction heats up as well.

On a cold day, turn up the heat by making your sweetheart a nice cup of hot cocoa or tea and snuggle up to a warm fire.

[17] Williams, L. E., & Bargh, J. A. (2008). Experiencing Physical Warmth Promotes Interpersonal Warmth. Science, 322(5901), 606-607.

12

let's talk about sex, baby

One of the most important parts of our relationships is often the most awkward and difficult to talk about. Sex is a loaded topic, and one that makes us feel vulnerable. Hoping your partner will read your mind isn't the best strategy. Research shows that the more you discuss sex openly, sharing your feelings and desires, the more likely you are to have a lot more (and better) sex.[18] This is particularly true the longer you have been together.

Be gentle with your feedback and open-minded to theirs. It takes two to tango, and even outside the bedroom, that conversation will increase your physical intimacy and closeness.

Set aside a night and share your thoughts about intimacy with each other.

[18] Montesi, J. L., Fauber, R. L., Gordon, E. A., & Heimberg, R. G. (2010). The specific importance of communicating about sex to couples' sexual and overall relationship satisfaction. Journal of Social and Personal Relationships.

13

no phone zone

As important as technology is to our lives, studies show that phones, social media, TV, and other distractions can be damaging to our relationships. Even if you don't answer your cell phone, simply receiving a notification is distracting to you and others around you.[19]

One study showed that simply placing your phone on the table during dinner significantly reduces the depth and intimacy of the discussion, **even if the phone is turned off.**[20] To truly connect, take away the tech; as you stretch to find new things to do, you will spend more quality time together and your relationship will grow.

For one week, turn off all electronics: TV, radio, internet, phones, social media, etc. The first day can be rough, but soon you'll look for creative, old-fashioned ways to have fun.

If you can't manage a full week, make sure you at least turn off your cell phone during your next dinner date. Check out some non-tech ways to have fun on the following page.

[19] Stothart, C., Mitchum, A., & Yehnert, C. (2015). The attentional cost of receiving a cell phone notification. Journal of Experimental Psychology: Human Perception and Performance, 41(4), 893-897.
[20] Przybylski, A. K., & Weinstein, N. (2012). Can you connect with me now? How the presence of mobile communication technology influences face-to-face conversation quality. Journal of Social and Personal Relationships.

1. Host a crafts night
2. Build a model airplane, rocket, train
3. Experiment with a chemistry set
4. Learn magic tricks
5. Scrapbooking
6. Perform karaoke, make up your own raps
7. Make a time capsule
8. Sew something – quilt, puppet, clothes
9. Play pool, ping pong, darts
10. Host a baking/cooking contest
11. Visit relatives
12. Make photo calendar/book
13. Visit a zoo, farm or aquarium
14. Play games, board games, cards, puzzles
15. Attend a demolition derby
16. Take a train ride
17. Visit the state fair
18. Have a picnic
19. Go to a dance show, ballet
20. Attend a concert – at a venue, free in the park
21. Visit the Humane Society
22. Go to a mystery escape room
23. Attend an air show
24. Visit the theater
25. Visit a museum or planetarium
26. Attend the circus
27. Take a class together, learn a language
28. Create a Build-a-Bear
29. Attend a pro/college/high school sports game: football, gymnastics, baseball, etc.
30. Attend a rodeo

14

hug it out

Giving a hug is such a kind and simple gesture. This physical expression actually makes us feel more loved, connected with others, happier and even healthier. In 2015, a study of 406 adults exposed to the cold virus showed that hugging could lessen their symptoms or prevent them from contracting the cold at all.

That's right— hugs literally boost your lover's immune system.[21] The more hugs, the better. Towards the end of your embrace, try the Brazilian tradition of breathing deeply through your nose and really take in everything about the experience.

Give your loved one a hug and hold on a little longer. Remember that with each hug you are showing your lover how much you want to be connected.

[21] Cohen, S., Janicki-Deverts, D., Turner, R. B., & Doyle, W. J. (2014). Does Hugging Provide Stress-Buffering Social Support? A Study of Susceptibility to Upper Respiratory Infection and Illness. Psychological Science.

15

get some perspective

We all have our fights—there's no such thing as a couple who doesn't. But what sets healthy relationships apart is our ability to grow from those conflicts. Researchers tracked 120 couples in declining marriages and asked half to write down each fight they shared with their partner from the perspective of a neutral third party.

The couples who saw the conflict from a different perspective began to succeed in their relationship, while those who didn't continued to fail.[22] Looking at the disagreement from another perspective allows a couple to see new alternatives and solutions to a problem.

When things have settled down after your next conflict, take a few minutes and write your thoughts from the perspective of a neutral party. Try and look at the conflict from several different perspectives, if possible.

[22] Finkel, E. J., Slotter, E. B., Luchies, L. B., Walton, G. M., & Gross, J. J. (2013). A Brief Intervention to Promote Conflict Reappraisal Preserves Marital Quality Over Time. Psychological Science.

16

fall in love... again?

Some say falling in love is easy. Strangely enough, there are 36 questions that prove just how easy it can be. In a 1997 study, researchers found a set of questions that would send people head over heels for one another. Participants set aside three nights for one month to spend 45 minutes answering these "self-disclosure" questions in sets of 12. The result? Sparks began to fly.[23]

For 45 minutes once a week, for three weeks, go over the questions on the following pages with your loved one. Discover just how much further you can fall in love with them as you deepen your connection.

[23] Aron, A., Melinat, E., Aron, E. N., Vallone, R. D., & Bator, R. J. (1997). The Experimental Generation of Interpersonal Closeness: A Procedure and Some Preliminary Findings. Personality and Social Psychology Bulletin.

1. Given the choice of anyone in the world, whom would you want as a dinner guest?

2. Would you like to be famous? In what way?

3. Before making a telephone call, do you ever rehearse what you are going to say? Why?

4. What would constitute a "perfect" day for you?

5. When did you last sing to yourself? To someone else?

6. If you were able to live to the age of 90 and retain either the mind or body of a 30-year-old for the last 60 years of your life, which would you want?

7. Do you have a secret hunch about how you will die?

8. Name 3 things you and your partner appear to have in common.

9. For what in your life do you feel most grateful?

10. If you could change anything about the way you were raised, what would it be?

11. Take 4 minutes and tell your partner your life story in as much detail as possible.

12. If you could wake up tomorrow having gained any quality or ability, what would it be?

13. If a crystal ball could tell you the truth about yourself, your life, the future or anything else, what would you want to know?

14. Is there something you've dreamed of doing for a long time? Why haven't you done it?

15. What is the greatest accomplishment of your life?

16. What do you value most in a friendship?

17. What is your most treasured memory?

18. What is your most terrible memory?

19. If you knew that in one year you would die suddenly, would you change anything about the way you are now living? Why?

20. What does friendship mean to you?

21. What roles do love and affection play in your life? Alternate sharing something you consider a positive characteristic of your partner. Share a total of five items.

22. How close is your family?

23. Do you feel your childhood was happier than most?

24. How do you feel about your relationship with your mother?

25. Make 3 true "we" statements each. For instance, "We are both in this room, feeling..."

26. Complete this sentence: "I wish I had someone with whom I could share..."

27. If you were going to become a close friend with your partner, please share what would be important for him or her to know.

28. Tell your partner what you like about them; be very honest this time, saying things that you might not say to someone you've just met.

29. Share with your partner an embarrassing moment in your life.

30. When did you last cry in front of another person? By yourself?

31. Tell your partner something that you like about them already.

32. What, if anything, is too serious to be joked about?

33. If you were to die this evening with no opportunity to communicate with anyone, what would you most regret not having told someone? Why haven't you told them yet?

34. Your house, containing everything you own, catches fire. After saving your loved ones and pets, you have time to safely make a final dash to save any one item. What would it be? Why?

35. Of all the people in your family, whose death would you find most disturbing? Why?

36. Share a personal problem and ask your partner's advice on how he or she might handle it. Also, ask your partner to reflect back to how you seemed to be feeling about the problem you have chosen.

How did it go?

17

take my hand

Remember that moment of excitement when you first slipped your palm into theirs? As our relationships progress, we take hand holding for granted, even though it's a powerful display of affection and expression of your love and commitment. Recently, researchers conducted a study on the importance of handholding. They actually electrically shocked women as they held hands with their spouses. MRI scans demonstrated that the women holding their partner's hand felt less pain from the same shock as women who had no hand to hold.[24]

Additionally, North Carolina researchers found that prior to giving a public speech, people who weren't allowed to touch and hold hands had blood pressure and heart rates that were nearly twice as high as those who held hands.[25] Holding hands can help us feel reassured and reminds us how lucky we are to be loved.

Go for a walk, reach for and hold on to your lover's hand, the way you did in those first few months. Tell them just how much you love holding their hand.

[24] Coan, J. A., Schaefer, H. S., & Davidson, R. J. (2006). Lending a Hand: Social Regulation of the Neural Response to Threat. Psychological Science.
[25] Grewen, K. M., Anderson, B. J., Girdler, S. S., & Light, K. C. (2003). Warm Partner Contact Is Related to Lower Cardiovascular Reactivity. Behavioral Medicine.

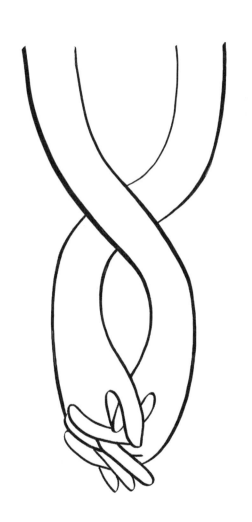

18

give a little

Giving, receiving, enjoying gifts, it doesn't matter—we love gifts no matter the occasion. But, research confirms that the types of gifts you give also make a difference. Giving an experience (event tickets, couple's massage, cooking class, etc.) brings more satisfaction than something tangible such as a new TV or clothes.[26]

If you plan to give something tangible, consider asking your partner what they want and then give your partner what they ask for. As the giver you feel better knowing that you are picking something out your partner really wants and the one receiving the gift perceives you as more loving and thoughtful.[27]

Give your partner the gift of an experience they really want. Better yet, pair it with a small, meaningful physical present, such as a college sweatshirt with tickets to a football game, a nice pan with cooking classes or a CD with concert tickets.

[26] Boven, L. V., & Gilovich, T. (2003). To Do or to Have? That Is the Question. Journal of Personality and Social Psychology.
[27] Zhang, Y., & Epley, N. (2012). Exaggerated, mispredicted, and misplaced: When "it's the thought that counts" in gift exchanges. Journal of Experimental Psychology: General, 141(4), 667-681.

19

talk some cents

Even bankers can acknowledge that money is a touchy subject in their relationship. It's often a minefield, and studies show that disagreements about finances are often the biggest reason relationships fail.[28] When we enter a relationship, we bring our own views and concerns about spending and saving, many of which we don't put into words.

These types of concerns are bound to surface during conflicts. Taking the time now to "talk some cents" is so important. Research shows that just talking about your feelings towards money strengthens the relationship.[29]

Get it all on paper. Spend a few minutes and independently complete the "money personality inventory" in the back of the book that clarifies your general thoughts and values regarding money. Then, sit down with your partner and discuss.

[28] Dew, J., Britt, S., & Huston, S. (2012). Examining the Relationship Between Financial Issues and Divorce. Family Relations.

[29] Washburn, Carolyn, and Darlene Christensen. 2008. Financial harmony: A key component of successful marriage relationship. The Forum for Family and Consumer Issues, 13 (1).

20

work it out

Couples who exercise together, stay together; it's a fact. Participating in high energy activities makes you look more attractive to your partner. Better yet, when you participate in high-energy activities together, you're happier and more connected (not to mention healthier)![30]

Out of all the ways we can get moving—biking, hiking, yoga, dancing, running, you name it—there's bound to be one you both enjoy. Be each other's biggest coach, teammate and fan. Then watch and see how becoming more fit together will help your relationship take incredible strides.

Share with each other the types of activities you enjoy most, then schedule a time to do physical activity together three times a week. Set goals and put them on the calendar.

[30] Aron, A., Norman, C. C., Aron, E. N., Mckenna, C., & Heyman, R. E. (2000). Couples' shared participation in novel and arousing activities and experienced relationship quality. Journal of Personality and Social Psychology, 78(2), 273-284.

21

worship together

If you're religious, one of the best ways to grow together is to worship together. No matter which religion you practice, commitment to a higher power together means a better commitment to each other. As your faith grows stronger by one another's side, so will your faith in your relationship.

As a side benefit, crazy (but awesome) as it seems, research shows a correlation between worshipping together and a good sex life. Couples who worshipped together were more satisfied with their sex life and felt the most loved and excited during lovemaking.[31]

The next time you worship together, take a few minutes afterward to tell your sweetheart how grateful you are to God for having them in your life.

[31] Fagan, P. F., Ph.D. (2016, Winter). Marriage, Worship, and Sexuality. The Family in America a Journal of Public Policy.

22

listen up

Men, this one's for you. We always want to be there for our loved one, and often that means more than just being there physically. Unfortunately, it's no secret that men tend to be worse listeners than women.

Research shows that women benefit significantly from being with men who are empathetic listeners. The good news for us men is that we benefit even more than women when we are sensitive and compassionate listeners. In fact, men even felt more love when they were good listeners.[32] Better listening is a win-win for both partners.

Set aside five minutes, look each other in the eyes and ask about the other person's day, and then, really listen. Put aside all distractions, ask questions and empathize with their situation.

[32] Jensen, J. F., Rauer, A. J., & Volling, B. (2013). A Dyadic View of Support in Marriage: The Critical Role of Men's Support Provision. Sex Roles.

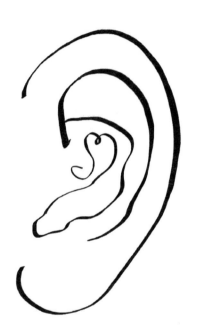

23

make the call

In the digital age, it's pretty convenient to communicate with your partner through texts, social media and more. But to be really close, nothing compares to hearing your loved one's voice.

Research shows that direct communication is seven times more effective than something digital.[33] Couples who call each other often reported feeling more certainty and commitment in their relationship than those who did not. A strong foundation of love is built with many small acts of connecting.

Call your sweetheart everyday, just to say hi and ask them how they are.

[33] Jin, B., & Peña, J. F. (2010). Mobile Communication in Romantic Relationships: Mobile Phone Use, Relational Uncertainty, Love, Commitment, and Attachment Styles. Communication Reports.

24

lock lips for love

Not counting pecks or cheek kisses—do you remember the last time you kissed your partner with passion? If its hard to remember, you're not alone. The longer we stay together, the fewer kisses we share. But remember when you used to kiss for hours?

Studies show kissing your lover more often and for longer creates higher levels of satisfaction and lower levels of stress; it can even lower your cholesterol.[34] One passionate smooch goes a long way!

Wrap your arms around your lover and tell them you want to give them a real kiss. Make sure it lasts longer than seven seconds.

[34] Floyd, K., Boren, J. P., Hannawa, A. F., Hesse, C., Mcewan, B., & Veksler, A. E. (2009). Kissing in Marital and Cohabiting Relationships: Effects on Blood Lipids, Stress, and Relationship Satisfaction. Western Journal of Communication.

25

the anchor of traditions

Why do we love traditions so much? What is it about repeating the same rituals year after year that gives us that warm and fuzzy feeling? According to a 2010 study from Northeastern, humans love predictability and stability so much that up to 93 percent of all our actions can be predicted ahead of time.[35] Traditions add meaning and predictability to relationships.

Whether you have date night every Friday night, eat the same Sunday meal together, attend the same event each year or even kiss each other good night in the same way— traditions and routines cement your relationship and make for lasting relationships for years to come.

Write down 3 traditions that you could start to help solidify your relationship.

---

[35] Song, C., Qu, Z., Blumm, N., & Barabasi, A. (2010). Limits of Predictability in Human Mobility. Science.

26

lighten up

The best relationships are the ones where couples are connected and vulnerable. When we hurt our partner (which we all do on occasion), we need to say sorry and reconcile.[36] Researchers at Erasmus University asked certain participants to think about a time when they forgave someone, while asking other participants to think about their grudges. Then, they asked participants to jump as high as they could.

Those who thought about forgiveness, on average jumped over 3 inches higher.[37] Forgiveness literally makes us feel lighter. Whether we are the person wronged or the wrongdoer, it is vital to repair the damage and connect again.

Think of one grudge you have been holding on to and let it go by explaining and sharing your pain with your partner, asking their forgiveness and then letting go for good.

[36] Song, C., Qu, Z., Blumm, N., & Barabasi, A. (2010). Limits of Predictability in Human Mobility. Science.

[37] Riek, B. M., Luna, L. M., & Schnabelrauch, C. A. (2013). Transgressors' guilt and shame: A longitudinal examination of forgiveness seeking. Journal of Social and Personal Relationships.

27

get in tune

We connect with music in a unique, emotional way. It plays a significant role in the strength of a relationship. Music actually impacts our brain circuits to enhance empathy, trust and cooperation.[38] Finding common interests in music is an important part in establishing the relationship in its early phases, and discovering "our song" can really anchor your love.[39]

Studies show that passion decreases over time in a relationship and music becomes less important. But rediscovering your favorite songs and finding new ones can spark a new flame. Not only does music help create connectedness, it releases endorphins which enhance our overall wellbeing and love for others.[40]

Find a new love song that you two can call your own. Even better, make it a tradition to find a new song each anniversary, birthday or other special occasion.

[38] Koelsch, S. (2013). From Social Contact to Social Cohesion—The 7 Cs. Music and Medicine.

[39] Boer, D., Fischer, R., Strack, M., Bond, M. H., Lo, E., & Lam, J. (2011). How Shared Preferences in Music Create Bonds Between People: Values as the Missing Link. Personality and Social Psychology Bulletin.

[40] Tarr, B., Launay, J., & Dunbar, R. I. (2014). Music and social bonding: "self-other" merging and neurohormonal mechanisms. Frontiers in Psychology Front. Psychol., 5.

28

a date
with nature

Sometimes we take for granted what's all around us. Forests, lakes, mountains, rivers—they offer more than endless natural beauty and possibility. Connecting with the great outdoors can actually enhance your love and closeness to your partner.[41]

One simple way is watching a sunrise or sunset with your loved one, even if it's in your own backyard. Other ways to get outside include bird watching, walking in the park, gardening, yard work, and hiking through national parks or deep into caves. Look into outdoor escapes big and small around you.

Go on a nature walk with your partner and watch a sunset or sit by a stream and just hold each other.

[41] Zelenski, J. M., Dopko, R. L., & Capaldi, C. A. (2015). Cooperation is in our nature: Nature exposure may promote cooperative and environmentally sustainable behavior. Journal of Environmental Psychology.

29

see the sacrifices

Having a successful relationship is about investment, compromise, and sometimes, self-sacrifice. It's important to remember just how much your partner has done and be grateful.

Studies showed that lovers who made a list of the things their loved one gave up to benefit the relationship had a stronger bond with each other. Even if they didn't share what they wrote, their relationship still benefitted.[42] When people focus on what their partner has invested into the relationship, they naturally become more committed.

Ask yourself, "Has my partner given up anything today for the sake of our relationship?" Then write it down. Make a list of 10 things that your partner has given up or sacrificed in the last week for the benefit of the relationship.

[42] Joel, S., Gordon, A. M., Impett, E. A., Macdonald, G., & Keltner, D. (2013). The Things You Do for Me: Perceptions of a Romantic Partner's Investments Promote Gratitude and Commitment. Personality and Social Psychology Bulletin.

Career Cat
PRIDE
Family Indian fitness
Food Guy
Friends
SLEEP free
Time
SPORTS CHANNEL

30

movie night magic

Maybe date night's become a drag or perhaps there's no date night at all. But even doing something simple such as watching a romantic movie can go a long way. In 2013, around 200 engaged or newlywed couples were placed into various groups. Two groups attended intense relationship workshops, another was tasked to watch and discuss one romantic movie a week for one month, and the last was the control group.

After monitoring for three years, the movie night group was just as effective at avoiding divorce as the workshop group, while the control group was twice as likely to break up. Bottom line: workshops can be expensive, but taking 15-30 minutes after movie night to share thoughts can cost little to nothing and yield the same results.[43]

Grab a blanket and a snack then curl up with your loved one for some quality movie time. Chat about the movie once it's over.

[43] Rogge, R. D., Cobb, R. J., Lawrence, E., Johnson, M. D., & Bradbury, T. N. (2013). Is skills training necessary for the primary prevention of marital distress and dissolution? A 3-year experimental study of three interventions. Journal of Consulting and Clinical Psychology.

31

do the little things

Every couple is different when it comes to work around the home. But if one partner feels like the other is not carrying their load, this can really cause problems for the relationship.[44] Everyone has certain household chores they don't mind doing and other things they can't stand. Discuss with your partner your various likes and dislikes, take a moment to reflect on your partner's contributions and be grateful for what he/she contributes.

Be willing to put in a little more effort doing the chores you don't mind doing. You will make yourself more indispensable to your lover as your relationship becomes more stable and secure.

Make a list of 20 household chores and then each of you rank them 1-10 from like to dislike. Share your list with each other and talk for 15 minutes about your feelings.

[44] Harryson, L., Strandh, M., & Hammarström, A. (2012). Domestic Work and Psychological Distress—What Is the Importance of Relative Socioeconomic Position and Gender Inequality in the Couple Relationship? PLoS ONE, 7(6).

32

pay some compliments

If you're human, you might not always feel so good about your body. Insecurity is natural, but how we feel about our appearance can have a severe impact on our relationship. However, our partner's words go a long way, and studies show that our partners see us as more beautiful than we see ourselves.

It's a phenomenon that affects both men and women, and studies show that talking about your ideal body type actually helps couples feel better about their bodies and be more realistic about body image. Trust your partner when they say, "You look great!", because that is truly what they see.[45] [46] [47]

Be grateful and give your loved one at least one compliment a day and see them smile. Make them feel beautiful and let them know they're loved. They'll return the favor!

[45] Markey, C. N., & Markey, P. M. (2006). Romantic Relationships and Body Satisfaction Among Young Women. J Youth Adolescence Journal of Youth and Adolescence.
[46] Gillen, M. M. & Markey, C. N. (2015). Body Image and Mental Health. In H.S. Friedman (Ed.), Encyclopedia of Mental Health, 2nd Edition. New York, New York, Elsevier.
[47] Markey, C. N., Markey, P. M., August, K. J., & Nave, C. S. (2015). Body Talk Improves Body Image Among Couples.

33

for love
& money

No one likes a cheapskate. In fact, research shows just the opposite. People perceive savers as sexy.[48] Researchers found that someone viewed as responsible with money was seen as more attractive, nicer, and more trustworthy. This perception stems from the notion of self control. If you can control your spending, you can probably control other harmful behaviors as well.[49]

It is also no big surprise that couples with higher credit scores are also more likely to remain in a committed relationship.[50] Just make sure that your frugality doesn't kill your spontaneity and fun.

Set aside some dollars for a future benefit, maybe an extravagant dinner, vacation, whatever you decide. Do so with automatic withdrawals or talk with a financial advisor.

[48] KOlson, J. G., & Rick, S. (n.d.). A Penny Saved is a Partner Earned: The Romantic Appeal of Savers. SSRN Electronic Journal SSRN Journal.

[49] Dokko, J., Li, G., & Hayes, J. (n.d.). Credit Scores and Committed Relationships. SSRN Electronic Journal SSRN Journal.

[50] Dokko, J., Li, G., & Hayes, J. (n.d.). Credit Scores and Committed Relationships. SSRN Electronic Journal SSRN Journal.

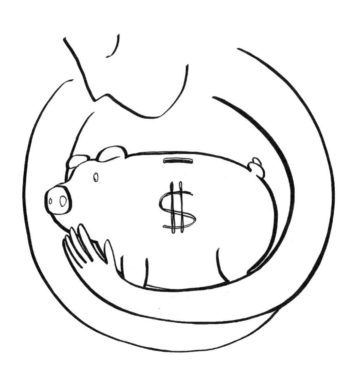

34

give an appreciation

Gratitude is proven to help couples stay together. Studies confirm that acknowledging someone's successes is even more powerful and meaningful to a relationship than supporting them in the difficult times (although you should do both!)[51]

As you give and receive compliments or "appreciations" from your partner, you improve your listening skills and grow closer as a couple. Look for opportunities to give "appreciations" at dinner, while driving, and especially after long absences. More gratitude equates to more secure relationships.

Step 1 – Look the other person in the eyes and ask, "Are you available?" You want to make sure the other person is ready to accept the appreciation.

Step 2 – When the receiver is ready, say, "One thing that I really appreciate about you is..." followed by one thing you like or appreciate about the other person.

Step 3 – The receiver then mirrors back the appreciation to the giver by saying, "So, what you appreciate about me is ..." Try to take in the compliment and see it from the other person's perspective.

[51] Barton, A. W., Futris, T. G., & Nielsen, R. B. (2015). Linking financial distress to marital quality: The intermediary roles of demand/withdraw and spousal gratitude expressions. Personal Relationships.

35

pillow talk

You have just done the wild thing, or maybe the same old thing—now what? Not surprisingly, people who spend more time showing affection after sex were more satisfied in their sex lives and happier in their relationship.

In fact, researchers have found that the time spent after sex is more important to the relationship than the sex itself, or the foreplay.[53] Sharing something as intimate as sex with your true love is amazing. Remember to spend a few minutes after to really solidify and appreciate your togetherness.

Cuddle up next to your partner for at least 15 minutes after you're intimate, and share a few words on how much you mean to one another. Spending this time together extends your intimacy and shows a great deal of affection and appreciation for your loved one.

[53] Denes, A. (2014). The Science of Pillow Talk - UConn Today.

a wink & a smile

As long as we are texting our sweethearts throughout the day, why not make it more personal by using emojis? Everyone loves a real smile, but brain research shows that even emoticons are processed in the occipitotemporal sites of the brain similar to how we process actual faces.[54]

Further research proves that emoticons can create a positive effect on enjoyment and improve personal interactions.[55] In fact, emoticons even make you appear more friendly and competent.[56] So why not send one in your next text?

Include a wink emoji or something fun in the next text to your lover. It's almost as good as the real thing.

[54] Churches, O., Nicholls, M., Thiessen, M., Kohler, M., & Keage, H. (2014). Emoticons in mind: An event-related potential study. Social Neuroscience.

[55] Huang, A. H., Yen, D. C., & Zhang, X. (2008). Exploring the potential effects of emoticons. Information & Management.

[56] Kalyanaraman, S. and Ivory, J. D. "The Face of Online Information Processing: Effects of Emoticons on Impression Formation, Affect, and Cognition in Chat Transcripts."

You are my ☀

👁 ♡ U 💋

37

share the love

People who volunteer are happier. In one study, people who serve often reported higher levels of happiness, life satisfaction, self esteem, a sense of control over life, better physical health and lower levels of depression.[57] Isn't that what we all want? Now imagine the benefits to your relationship if you provide service together. It only takes 1-2 hours a week to receive all these benefits that come from volunteering.[58]

Discover a type of service you'd both like to do, contact an organization you both value, then get involved. Whether you are serving food to the homeless, spending time with the elderly, or teaching children to read, jump in and enjoy spending this time serving others at least once a week.

[57] Thoits, P.A. and Hewitt, L.N. (2001) "Volunteer Work and Well-Being." Journal of Health and Social Behavior, 42(2): 115-131.
[58] Lum, T.Y. and Lightfoor, E. (2005) "The Effects of Volunteering on the Physical and Mental Health of Older People." Research on Aging, 27(1): 31-55.

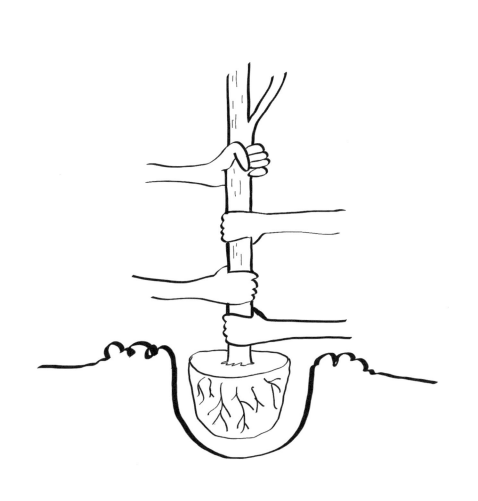

38

get in touch

As human beings, we're wired to enjoy the touch of those we care about—it's electrifying. For lovers, research has now shown that slow, sensitive strokes activate the part of the brain associated with emotions. These deep, powerful feelings of affection drive how we rate and perceive the quality of the relationship, and the more these feelings are triggered, the better.

Giving a simple massage for 15 minutes lowers stress hormones and releases Oxytocin, a hormone that creates social bonding.[59] The great news is that the person giving the massage and the receiver both benefit from the touch!

Lay down, turn on some soft music and give your sweetheart a 10-15-minute massage.

[59] Morhenn, V. B., Beavin Haider, L. E., & Zak, P. J. (n.d.). Massage increases oxytocin and reduces adrenocorticotropin hormone in humans. Alternative Therapies in Health and Medicine 18(6):11-8.

39

step in the right direction

If you want to be going in the same direction in your relationship metaphorically, you should start by doing it literally. Studies show that couples are happier and more stable if they drive the same way to work, walk the same way in the hallway, or even both take the subway in the same direction. Physically moving in the same direction helps you feel connected and stable.[60]

Make a simple list of the things you do in the same direction as your partner vs. things that you do in a different direction. Become aware of your physical surroundings and make simple changes so that you are more connected in your relationship. Look for ways to move in the same direction and your relationship will be more stable.

[60] Huang, X. (., Dong, P., Dai, X., & Wyer, R. S. (2012). Going my way? The benefits of travelling in the same direction. Journal of Experimental Social Psychology, 48(4), 978-981.

40

hit the road

Sharing experiences together is how we develop and strengthen our love. Whether it's a spontaneous road trip to nowhere or romantic couples retreat, this exciting bonding experience can fuel your feelings of love for one another.[61] Break away from the world for two or three nights, and see what adventures you end up sharing together.

Plan a great escape with your loved one and rekindle the flame. Make sure when you plan your getaway to have the mutual goal in mind to renew your sense of love and affection toward each other.

[61] Nawijn, J., Marchand, M. A., Veenhoven, R., & Vingerhoets, A. J. (2010). Vacationers Happier, but Most not Happier After a Holiday. Applied Research Quality Life Applied Research in Quality of Life, 5(1), 35-47.

41

the three minute jar

In a broad study about being proactive, researchers found that random, spontaneous activities can help improve your relationship.[62] Here's an idea that may help. Fill a jar with random activities and set it next to your side of the bed. Each week choose one activity from the jar. Once you have done the activity, move the jar to the other person's side of the bed, and it is now their turn to choose an item from the jar.

If you skip a week, no big deal! Switch the jar to the other side and keep going. If you are not in the mood to do the activity, choose another. No pressure, no guilt. Have fun and try to connect!

Read a random note from the jar or make one up. Spend up to 3 minutes on each exercise, and see your relationship improve while having fun for years.

[62] Huei, W. C., & Sharon, K. P. (2013). Thinking and Acting in Anticipation: A Review of Research on Proactive Behavior. Advances in Psychological Science, 21(4), 679-700.

- Give each other an appreciation

- Hold each other for 3 minutes

- Share a fun memory

- Give a back/head/foot massage

- Watch a funny video clip together

- Share a 7-second kiss

- Eat a small treat together

- Kneel and pray together holding hands

- Make herbal tea/cocoa together

- Slow dance or snuggle to a song

- Kiss each other in 7 different places

- Say "I love you" and look in their eyes for 30 seconds

let's get digital, digital

We've talked about how detaching yourself from technology can strengthen your relationship. How about using it to your advantage? While phone calls have been proven to be better than texts, for some younger couples, sending romantic texts and emails can be even more effective than talking on the phone.[63]

No matter your age, whether you are a texter, emailer or snapchatter, take a moment to let your lover know much you care. Sometimes slowing down and writing a romantic message to your lover can have a huge impact for good on the relationship.

Send your lover a surprise text or email expressing your love and appreciation to them.

[63] Wells, T. M., & Dennis, A. R. (2016). To email or not to email: The impact of media on psychophysiological responses and emotional content in utilitarian and romantic communication. Computers in Human Behavior, 54, 1-9.

43

surprise me

Who doesn't like a surprise? Spontaneity is the spice of life. When people become bored in their relationships, they become less attracted to one another.[64] Surprise boosts our dopamine levels which simultaneously increases our attraction and excitement, intensifying our emotions by about 400%.

Whether it's a love note, an unexpected invitation to get intimate, lipstick "I heart U" on the mirror, a surprise gift, or even a pillow fight, do something spontaneous to spice up your love.

Surprise your partner with a love note on their pillow or arrange for a surprise delivery of their favorite thing. Be creative!

[64] Tsapelas, I., Aron, A., & Orbuch, T. (2009). Marital Boredom Now Predicts Less Satisfaction 9 Years Later. Psychological Science, 20(5), 543-545.communication. Computers in Human Behavior, 54, 1-9.

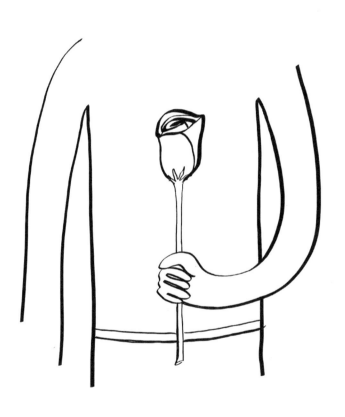

44

looking forward to you

Just like surprises, having something fun or exciting to look forward to can be immensely strengthening to a relationship. Giving your spouse the gift of anticipation will be an ongoing reminder of your love for each other.[65]

It can be planning a getaway together, starting a "12 Days of Christmas" gift giving tradition, or even setting aside one night a week to be together—each creates this anticipation that binds lovers together even tighter.

Plan a random monthly gift or surprise for your sweetheart. You can even sign up online at special websites and have something sent each month to your honey.

[65] Tsapelas, I., Aron, A., & Orbuch, T. (2009). Marital Boredom Now Predicts Less Satisfaction 9 Years Later. Psychological Science, 20(5), 543-545.

45

something sweet for someone sweet

We all know that giving someone chocolate is a way to show affection and love. No big surprise that science has proven there is something wonderful about chocolate and most people feel better while eating it.[66]

We often use terms of endearment such as sweetie, honey and sugar to express how we feel about our lovers. Why not tell your lover how sweet they are by giving them a sweet treat?

Give your sweetie a specialty chocolate bar or favorite treat and write them a simple note telling them how sweet they really are.

[66] Michener, W., & Rozin, P. (1994). Pharmacological versus sensory factors in the satiation of chocolate craving. Physiology & Behavior.

46

learn together, stay together

You're never too old to learn something new. Why not share this gratifying experience with someone you love while growing your relationship? With so many options available in almost any community, you're bound to find one you're both interested in.

Try a cooking, sewing, or painting class, or maybe take up stargazing or watching Discovery Channel together. Any time you choose a way to expand your minds together, you are additionally elevating your relationship.[67]

Sign up for a class or find a new hobby for you to do together.

[67] Field, J. (2011). Is Lifelong Learning Making a Difference? Research-Based Evidence on the Impact of Adult Learning. Second International Handbook of Lifelong Learning, 887-897.

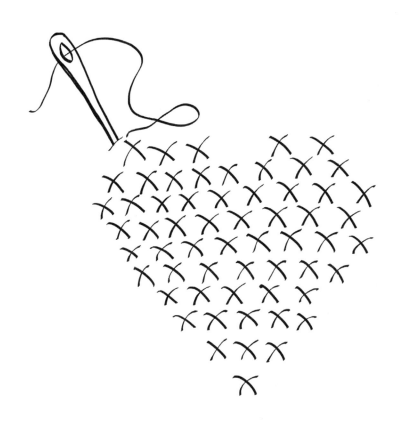

47

fun with footsies

A great way to spice up your love life is by sharing secret moments. When you and your partner engage in secret intimate behavior, you create a spark that's not only fun but also really connective.

Maybe it's a stolen kiss around the corner, or footsies under the dinner table. These public yet private moments you share can be a fun, carefree source of newfound intimacy – just don't get caught.[68]

Next time you are out to dinner, or in a group with other people, get a little crazy and look for a moment when you can romantically touch without people catching you.

[68] Wegner, D. M., Lane, J. D., & Dimitri, S. (1994). The allure of secret relationships. Journal of Personality and Social Psychology, 66(2), 287-300.

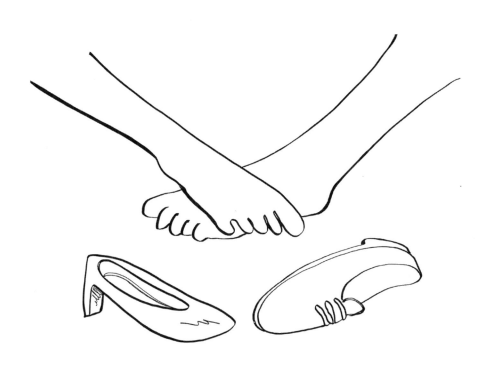

48

that's our stuff

Once you start living with someone, you begin to accumulate a lot of things together over the years. Interestingly enough, the stuff we purchase says a lot about the strength of our relationship.

Researchers looked at the items couples shared and displayed in their homes and found that couples who bought more things together felt closer and more committed to one another, as well as experienced less conflict.[69]

Bring your lover along for the next shopping spree. Find something you both like for your home (art, furniture, decoration, etc.) and buy it together. Put it in your house for all to see, and call it "ours."

[69] Lohmann, A., Arriaga, X. B., & Goodfriend, W. (2003). Close relationships and placemaking: Do objects in a couple's home reflect couplehood? Personal Relationships, 10(3), 437-450.

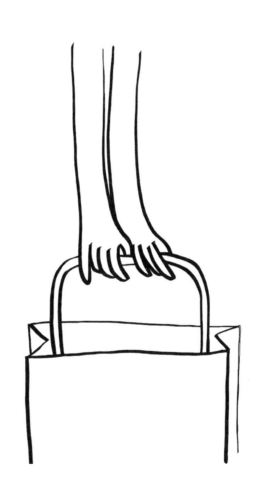

49

"tell me
i'm awesome"

When you're about to perform a potentially challenging task, research shows that if you visualize a random time you succeeded, you perform 2 $\frac{1}{2}$ times better. In contrast, when you think about times when you failed, you perform worse when trying to solve stressful problems.[70]

Use this knowledge to your advantage in your relationship. You can support your sweetheart by simply reminding them of a time they were spectacular. They will rise to the occasion.

Before your next big event or task, ask your spouse to reflect on a time when you were at your best and then have them share that memory with you.

[70] Cable, D., Lee, J. J., Gino, F., & Staats, B. R. (n.d.). How Best-Self Activation Influences Emotions, Physiology and Employment Relationships. SSRN Electronic Journal SSRN Journal.

50

a good thing takes work

One of the best ways to keep your love moving in the right direction is to keep learning about how to improve your relationship. "Lovemaking" is much more than what happens in the bedroom; it is an ongoing process, and the road to make it better never ends.

Love can be very fragile or immeasurably strong depending on how much you put into it. The more you invest in your relationship the more you will be happy, healthy and in love.

Check out the list on the following page of ideas that can help you continue your quest to become a stronger and happier couple.

- Interview marriage counselors and therapists. You don't necessarily have to get therapy, but it almost always helps to get good ideas and suggestions from these professionals. Ask them to give you a tip or assignment – then do it.

- Watch Ted Talks on relationships together or attend relationship conferences.

- Go to a couple's workshop together.

- Read relationship books.

- Follow a relationship blog and spend time on the internet researching your own tips.

- Be sure to visit our love50ways.com and our Facebook page (facebook.com/love50ways) for on-going relationship advice!

Purdue Money Personality Inventory

Read each scenario, and then circle the statement that best describes how you would respond to the situation. At the end, tally up your results and find the personality closest to yours.

1. *You're thinking about balancing your checkbook.*
    A. You personally enter each check, keep track of the balance, and reconcile the statement every month.
    B. You seldom know your exact bank balance.
    C. You frequently have to call up the bank to find out your bank balance.
    D. You keep a large overdraft protection and don't worry about it.

2. *You think you are overdue for a raise.*
    A. You double your efforts, get to work earlier, and work better and faster.
    B. You think it over and decide to wait and see what happens at the next salary review.
    C. You tell your boss you want a raise.
    D. You complain to your friends about being unappreciated and start thinking about getting another job.

3. *Your daughter wants a $100 prom dress. You feel $60 would be more appropriate, but she persists.*
    A. To avoid an argument, you give in and let her charge it.
    B. You work out a plan so she can earn the money or pay you back for a part of the purchase price.
    C. You go shopping with her and take charge of the selection process. She ends up with a $200 dress.
    D. You start feeling sentimental and nostalgic and she talks you into the $100 dress.

4. *Your 5-year-old car is not yet paid for, but it is beginning to have mechanical problems. You cannot afford a new car.*

    A.   You get a consolidation loan to lower your monthly payments for other bills and trade in the car on a model that projects a successful image.

    B.   After comparison shopping, you buy the best you can afford.

    C.   You can't decide, so you procrastinate until it breaks down.

    D.   You decide you have to have a car and you close the deal in one afternoon.

5. *You have just unexpectedly inherited $50,000 from your aunt's estate. You have no children. How will you spend (or save) it?*

    A.   You buy clothes, furs, an automobile or something flamboyant that will amaze all your friends.

    B.   You buy expensive gifts for yourself and plan a wonderful vacation cruise with your favorite friends.

    C.   You deposit the money in the bank and are happy that you can loan it to friends who need it.

    D.   You seek the advice of an accountant and lawyer and set up an investment portfolio, putting the rest into a living trust.

6. *You have just unexpectedly inherited $50,000 from your aunt's estate. You have four children. How will you spend (or save) it?*

    A.   You set up trust funds for your children so they will not be able to get the money until they are 30 years old.

    B.   You buy a bigger house and throw a party.

    C.   You hire an investment counselor and start figuring out ways to corner the soybean market so you can make it really big.

    D.   You have no idea, but you figure something will occur to you after your talk it over with your friends. What's the rush?

7. *You have a 10-year-old daughter who shows signs of being highly gifted in auto mechanics.*

    A.   You don't see any reason why she should not pursue science and also excel in other areas, so you push her to develop her musical ability too.

    B.   You start a college tuition savings plan, but make only occasional deposits.

    C.   You think she's a great kid.

    D.   You hire a private tutor, brag about her at every opportunity, and start selecting which college she will attend.

8. *You just bought a house that is a fixer-upper, knowing that in a few years it will need a new roof.*
   A. You figure out what a new roof will cost in five years, divide that by sixty and start setting aside money every month to cover the cost, so when the time comes you can pay cash and get a better deal.
   B. You may not even be in this house in five years, so why worry about it now?
   C. A house is an investment. You plan to make cosmetic improvements and sell the house in three years. Let the new owners worry about the roof.
   D. For the same monthly outlay you decide to put in a swimming pool, which is a lot more fun than a roof.

9. *Where are your important family documents such as health and medical records, insurance policies, tax returns, deeds of trust, contracts for auto and furniture purchases, and instruction booklets for appliances?*
   A. You're not exactly sure where they are right now, but you could probably find them.
   B. You don't keep files on everything; if you ever need a copy of those things in an emergency, you would call somebody.
   C. It's not your management style to deal with trivial details; you have delegated this to someone else.
   D. You know where they are, and have a system for keeping them up-to-date.

10. *You are returning home from a committee meeting and your car is broadsided when the other driver disregards a stop sign.*
    A. You always know where your insurance policies are, what the coverage is, and when each policy expires.
    B. You don't have any insurance or it's lapsed.
    C. You know you have insurance, but you have misplaced the policies.
    D. You leave all such details up to your insurance broker.

11. *You receive a notice from the IRS stating you have been selected for an audit.*
    A. You know exactly what you paid in federal income tax last year.
    B. You didn't file your return or you usually file late.
    C. You filed a return, but you don't know where it is.
    D. You are in a dispute with the IRS.

12. *In your opinion, it's better to give than to receive.*

    A.   You have a budget for gift giving and keep within it.

    B.   You love to buy gifts for people. You charge most gift purchases and don't keep track.

    C.   You seldom buy gifts, but when you do, you don't go overboard.

    D.   Because you have expensive tastes, people enjoy receiving gifts from you. You don't keep track of how much you spend annually, but it's probably too much.

13. *Vacations are nice, when you have time for them.*

    A.   You haven't had a vacation in more than two years. When you do, it's to a first-class hotel, and you take work with you.

    B.   Although having fun is not a high priority with you, if you do have a vacation, you plan it, save for it, and do not go over your budget.

    C.   You usually don't take planned vacations; you just go places with your friends when someone else suggests it.

    D.   You love vacations. You may go on short trips, but you don't know what you spend and don't have a specific amount budgeted. You sure have a lot of fun.

14. *You have been passed over for a promotion.*

    A.   You don't say anything, but your withdrawn attitude lets everyone know you have been wronged. Inwardly, you feel there is something wrong with you.

    B.   It's not pleasant, but it isn't worth getting upset about.

    C.   You have a good cry, or storm about it to your friends for an evening, then gradually get over it and go on with your life.

    D.   You are mortally offended, and you immediately lay plans to find another position with a competing company.

15. *Financial advisers say you should have a written plan for your financial goals covering the next five years.*

    A.   When your next deal "hits big" it's going to make you rich. That, in a nutshell, is your whole plan: to strike it rich.

    B.   You have written goals and follow them carefully.

    C.   You have written goals, but don't follow them.

    D.   You haven't really given it much thought.

16. *You have just purchased a new car. When you get home and look over the contract again, you discover that you have been overcharged $100.*

    A.   You decide to forget it.

    B.   You decide to call the auto dealer to point out the mistake.

    C.   You get depressed about your own stupidity and the innate dishonesty of people.

    D.   You get furious and call up the salesman and yell at him. Later on you think of some thing really clever that you wish you had said.

17. *Keeping records of tax deductions:*

    A.   You have a system for keeping track of medical and other tax deductions, and you follow it to the letter.

    B.   You have a system but don't keep it up.

    C.   You don't have a system, but you think it's a good idea to have one.

    D.   You let your accountant, spouse, or tax adviser worry about that.

18. *You and your spouse:*

    A.   You make all the important money decisions and like it that way.

    B.   It always seems that your spouse doesn't care about money management, but you seem unable to change things, even though you nag.

    C.   You let your spouse take care of the money. Why bother yourself?

    D.   You get depressed about the future; there are so many things that could go wrong, and your spouse seems unaware of how important it is to plan meticulously.

19. *Attitudes toward housing cost:*

    A.   You never spend more than 35 percent of your income for housing costs.

    B.   You may not be able to afford to live in your present house, but it's important for the kids' sake to grow up in a nice neighborhood. The house will probably appreciate.

    C.   You don't care about your surroundings that much, so where you live is not crucially important to you personally.

    D.   It's important to live in a fine neighborhood if you want to be a part of the right social circles and be a success. You will spend whatever that takes.

20. *Saving:*

    A.   You save a specific amount from every pay period.

    B.   You opened a savings account some time ago and made a few deposits, but it's inactive right now.

    C.   You haven't thought about it seriously.

    D.   You don't save right now. All your money is earmarked for a big deal or big purchase.

21. *Which reflects your basic attitude about clothing?*

    A.   Looks and fashion first, quality second, cost third.

    B.   I don't know what I want until I see it, and if I don't have the money, I charge it.

    C.   A few high-quality clothes are a good investment.

    D.   Clothes aren't that big a deal.

22. *Of the following careers, which would you prefer if the salaries were all equal?*

    A.   Accountant, lab analyst, or editor.

    B.   Sales manager, actor, or rock singer.

    C.   Photographer, mechanic, or school counselor.

    D.   Senator, inventor, or corporation president.

23. *How would you describe the work area you presently control?*

    A.   A place for everything and everything in its place.

    B.   Cluttered and disorganized, but comfortable.

    C.   Photographs, plants, mementos reflecting me.

    D.   Functional, impersonal, effective.

24. *Which of the following is most true of you at work?*

    A.   You have trouble getting to work on time.

    B.   You arrive early and stay late. You're a workhorse.

    C.   You spend time chatting, socializing.

    D.   Your work is your life.

KEY

	Choleric	Sanguine	Melancholy	Phlegmatic
1.	D	C	A	B
2.	C	D	A	B
3.	C	D	B	A
4.	A	D	B	C
5.	A	B	D	C
6.	C	B	A	D
7.	D	B	A	C
8.	C	D	A	B
9.	C	A	D	B
10.	D	C	A	B
11.	D	C	A	B
12.	D	B	A	C
13.	A	D	B	C
14.	D	C	A	B
15.	A	C	B	D
16.	B	D	C	A
17.	D	B	A	C
18.	A	B	D	C
19.	D	B	A	C
20.	D	B	A	C
21.	A	B	C	D
22.	D	B	A	C
23.	D	C	A	B
24.	D	C	B	A

Choleric:

Cholerics are driven and set financial goals. Nothing gets between them and accomplishing what they set out to do. However, Cholerics need to remember their spouses in their financial goals, and not leave them out of important matters—even if this means slowing down to make sure their spouses are involved.

Sanguine:

Sanguines are generous and social. They usually find themselves in careers in sales and other occupations dealing with people, but can tend to be overspenders. While frugality may not be their strong point, Sanguines can help a frugal spouse feel less stressed by filling life with enjoyment.

Melancholy:

Melancholies are perfectionists. This personality knows where they stand financially and are very talented with their budgets. However, Melancholies must be cautious to not let imperfections in financial situations get the best of them.

Phlegmatic:

Phlegmatics are masters of contentment. They know how to live within their means and do not like spending more than needed. Frugality can be a great attribute, but Phlegmatics must try to overcome their fear of spending, and avoid being cheap.

Acknowledgments

Many people helped me get the book designed and produced.
Special thanks to:

Sarah Steenland - Illustrations
Suzanne King - Book Design
Heather Baldock - Editor
Michael Driggs - Production
Phil Smallwood, Steve Driggs - Design Concepts
Paragon Press - Printing